The AI millionaire Guide to making money online using AI

Caleb smith

Certainly! There are various online writing jobs that you can do to make money. These opportunities cater to different skill levels and interests, so you can find one that suits your expertise and schedule. Below are some popular online writing jobs:

1. Content Writing: Content writers create articles, blog posts, website content, and other written materials for businesses and individuals. This job requires strong writing skills, research abilities, and the ability to tailor content to specific audiences and industries.

2. Copywriting: Copywriters specialize in creating persuasive and engaging content for advertising, marketing, and promotional materials. They often work on crafting compelling headlines, product descriptions, email campaigns, and social media content.

3. Technical Writing: Technical writers produce instructional and informational content for complex subjects, such as software manuals, technical guides, and documentation. This role requires the ability to explain technical concepts in a clear and understandable manner.

4. Creative Writing: If you have a flair for storytelling and creativity, you can explore opportunities in creative writing. This may include writing fiction, poetry, short stories, and even scriptwriting for videos or podcasts.

5. Ghostwriting: Ghostwriters are hired to write content on behalf of others, typically without receiving public credit. They work on a variety of projects, such as books, speeches, articles, and blog posts.

6. Academic Writing: Academic writers create research papers, essays, theses, and other scholarly content for students and researchers. A strong understanding of academic formatting and referencing styles is essential for this role.

7. Resume Writing: Resume writers help job seekers create compelling and professional resumes to increase their chances of landing interviews.

8. Editing and Proofreading: If you have an eye for detail and excellent language skills, you can offer editing and proofreading services to writers and businesses.

9. Translation: If you are proficient in multiple languages, you can work as an online translator to translate written content from one language to another.

10. Freelance Blogging: Some websites pay freelance bloggers to write guest posts or contribute regular content on specific topics.

To find online writing jobs, you can explore various platforms and websites that connect writers with clients. Some popular freelance marketplaces for writers include Upwork, Freelancer, Fiverr, and Guru. Additionally, some job boards and websites specifically cater to writing opportunities, such as ProBlogger and FreelanceWriting.

CONTENT WRITING

When starting, consider creating a portfolio showcasing your best work, as it will help you demonstrate your skills and attract potential clients. Building a reputation as a reliable and talented writer can lead to more opportunities and higher-paying gigs in the long run. Remember to set competitive rates while also valuing your skills and time appropriately. With dedication and persistence, you can build a successful online writing career and make money doing what you love.

Content writing using AI can be a lucrative opportunity for individuals looking to make money online. AI technology, such as language models like GPT-3, can assist writers in generating high-quality content efficiently. Here's a detailed overview of how you can leverage AI for content writing and monetize your skills:

1. Develop your writing skills: Before utilizing AI for content writing, it's crucial to hone your writing abilities. Focus on improving your grammar, vocabulary, and overall writing style. This will help you provide valuable input to the AI model and ensure the content's quality.

2. Familiarize yourself with AI language models: Explore various AI language models available in the market, such as GPT-3, GPT-4, or other similar technologies. Understand their capabilities, features, and limitations. This knowledge will help you determine how to best leverage AI for content generation.

3. Choose a platform or tool: Several platforms and tools offer AI-powered content writing services. Examples

include OpenAI's GPT-3 Playground, ChatGPT API, Copy.ai, and Conversion.ai. Assess different platforms to find the one that aligns with your requirements, budget, and target audience.

4. Identify your niche: Determine your area of expertise or interest. Focusing on a specific niche allows you to develop subject matter expertise and attract clients or readers who are interested in that niche. Whether it's technology, travel, finance, health, or any other field, specializing can make you more valuable as a content writer.

5. Generate content ideas and outlines: Use AI tools to generate content ideas, article outlines, or headlines. These tools can provide you with a starting point or help you overcome writer's block. You can input a brief description or keywords, and the AI model will generate potential ideas, saving you time and effort.

6. Collaborate with AI for content creation: AI language models can assist in drafting content. You can provide the AI model with a prompt, such as a specific topic, and it will generate a draft for you. However, keep in mind that

AI-generated content may require manual editing and human touch to ensure accuracy and coherence.

7. Optimize content for SEO: Understanding search engine optimization (SEO) is essential for content writers. AI tools can assist in identifying relevant keywords, optimizing content structure, and improving readability. SEO-optimized content can attract more traffic to websites and increase your chances of getting hired for writing assignments.

8. Offer content writing services: Once you have a portfolio of well-crafted content, you can start offering your services as a content writer. Create a professional website or utilize freelance platforms to showcase your skills, attract clients, and secure writing projects. Networking and marketing your services through social media channels can also help in building your client base.

9. Monetize your content: There are multiple ways to monetize your content writing skills:

- Freelancing: Join freelancing platforms like Upwork, Fiverr, or Freelancer.com to find clients who are looking for content writers. Bid on relevant projects and build a reputation for delivering high-quality content on time.

- Blogging: Create your own blog or contribute articles to established blogs in your niche. Monetize your blog through advertising, sponsored content, affiliate marketing, or by offering premium content or services.

- Content marketplaces: Platforms like Medium, Substack, or Vocal provide opportunities to publish your content and earn money based on views, subscriptions, or reader contributions.

- E-books and digital products: Leverage your writing skills to create ebooks, online courses, or other digital products. Sell them through platforms like Amazon Kindle Direct Publishing or your website.

- Content writing agencies: Apply to content writing agencies or digital marketing companies that outsource writing projects. These agencies often have a

continuous need for content writers and can provide a steady flow of work.

10. Stay updated and adapt: AI technology is continuously evolving, and new tools and platforms will emerge. Stay updated with the latest trends and developments in AI-powered content writing. Adapt your skills and strategies accordingly to remain competitive in the field.

Remember, while AI can streamline content generation, human creativity, critical thinking, and editing skills are still essential for producing exceptional content. Combining the power of AI with your unique insights and expertise will enable you to create valuable content and monetize your content writing abilities effectively.

COPYWRITING

Copywriting is the art and science of writing persuasive and compelling content with the goal of promoting a product, service, or idea. With the advancement of AI technology, there are several ways in which you can leverage AI to make money from copywriting. Here's a detailed overview of the process:

1. Understand the Basics of Copywriting: Before using AI for copywriting, it's important to have a solid understanding of copywriting principles. Familiarize yourself with different copywriting techniques, such as creating attention-grabbing headlines, structuring persuasive arguments, and understanding your target audience.

2. Utilize AI-Powered Writing Tools: AI-powered writing tools like OpenAI's GPT-3 or similar platforms can assist you in generating high-quality copy. These tools use machine learning algorithms to analyze vast amounts of text data and generate human-like content. You can input brief or specific instructions and receive well-written drafts that you can edit and refine.

3. Enhance Product Descriptions: AI can help you write engaging and persuasive product descriptions. By analyzing customer reviews, competitor descriptions, and other relevant data, AI can generate product descriptions that highlight the unique selling points and benefits of a product. This can help increase conversions and sales for online businesses.

4. Develop Email Campaigns: Email marketing is a powerful tool for businesses, and AI can assist you in crafting effective email campaigns. AI can help generate subject lines, personalize content based on customer data, and suggest compelling calls-to-action. These automated processes can save time and optimize your email marketing efforts.

5. Create Social Media Content: AI can be used to generate engaging social media posts for platforms like Facebook, Instagram, and Twitter. By analyzing trending topics, customer preferences, and previous successful campaigns, AI can generate attention-grabbing headlines, captions, and social media content that resonate with your target audience.

6. Offer AI-Powered Copywriting Services: Position yourself as an AI-powered copywriter and offer your services to businesses and individuals. You can use AI tools to generate initial drafts and then apply your expertise to refine and polish the copy. Many businesses are willing to pay a premium for well-crafted, persuasive content that drives results.

7. Provide AI Copy Editing and Proofreading: AI can also be used to assist in the editing and proofreading process. AI-powered tools can analyze grammar, punctuation, spelling, and style, helping you ensure that your copy is error-free and coherent. By offering editing services enhanced by AI, you can provide high-quality copy to clients.

8. Develop AI Chatbot Scripts: Chatbots are becoming increasingly popular for customer support and engagement. As an AI copywriter, you can create conversational scripts for AI-powered chatbots, ensuring that they provide helpful, engaging, and persuasive responses to customer queries. This requires a deep understanding of customer needs and effective communication.

9. Continuous Learning and Adaptation: AI technology is constantly evolving, so it's crucial to stay updated with the latest advancements. Regularly explore new AI-powered writing tools and techniques, experiment with different approaches, and adapt your copywriting strategies

accordingly. This will help you maintain a competitive edge and deliver valuable services to clients.

Remember, while AI can assist in generating copy, it's essential to add a human touch to ensure the final output is of the highest quality. Combining AI capabilities with your creative thinking and expertise as a copywriter will allow you to provide unique value to clients and monetize your skills effectively.

TECHNICAL WRITING

Making money from technical writing using AI can be achieved through various avenues. Here's a detailed breakdown of how you can leverage AI to monetize your technical writing skills:

1. Content Creation: AI can assist in generating technical content, which can save time and effort. You can use AI-powered tools like language models to generate drafts or outlines for your technical documents. These tools can provide suggestions, correct grammar and spelling errors, and even help with sentence structuring. By using AI to streamline the content creation process, you can increase

your productivity and take on more writing projects, thereby earning more money.

2. Editing and Proofreading: AI can be a valuable tool for editing and proofreading technical documents. Automated grammar and spell checkers can help you identify and correct errors more efficiently. Additionally, AI-based style and readability analyzers can provide insights on improving the clarity and coherence of your writing. By utilizing AI-powered editing tools, you can enhance the quality of your technical writing, which can lead to higher-paying gigs and repeat clients.

3. Translation Services: Technical writing often requires translating documents from one language to another. AI language models, such as machine translation tools, can assist in translating technical content accurately and quickly. By offering translation services with the help of AI, you can cater to a broader audience and tap into international markets, expanding your potential client base and revenue streams.

4. Writing Assistance Tools: AI can act as a virtual writing assistant, helping you generate ideas, structure

your content, and optimize it for SEO. Writing assistance tools can analyze existing content, recommend keywords, and provide suggestions for improving the overall quality of your writing. These tools can be especially useful for creating SEO-friendly technical articles and blog posts, which can attract more clients and increase your earning potential.

5. Technical Documentation Automation: Many companies require extensive technical documentation for their products or services. AI-powered tools can automate the creation of technical manuals, user guides, FAQs, and other documentation. By leveraging AI in this process, you can streamline documentation creation, reduce time and effort, and potentially take on more clients. This efficiency gain allows you to complete more projects and generate more income.

6. Training and E-Learning Content: AI can be utilized to create interactive and engaging training materials and e-learning content. By incorporating AI-driven technologies like chatbots or virtual assistants, you can develop interactive training modules that provide on-demand assistance to learners. Creating such valuable and

interactive training content can attract clients looking to enhance their employee training programs, resulting in potential revenue streams.

7. AI-Powered Content Marketing: Utilizing AI in content marketing can help you attract more clients and increase your visibility as a technical writer. AI tools can analyze trends, identify popular topics, and suggest content ideas that resonate with your target audience. By leveraging AI to optimize your content marketing strategy, you can drive more traffic to your website, increase your online presence, and attract higher-paying clients.

8. Consulting and Advisory Services: With AI becoming increasingly integrated into technical writing processes, you can offer consulting and advisory services to businesses and individuals looking to adopt AI tools for their writing needs. You can provide guidance on selecting the right AI tools, implementing automated workflows, and optimizing their technical writing processes. By positioning yourself as an AI-savvy technical writing expert, you can command higher consulting fees and create additional revenue streams.

It's important to note that while AI can assist in various aspects of technical writing, human expertise and creativity are still essential. AI tools should be seen as aids rather than replacements for human writers. By leveraging AI effectively, you can enhance your technical writing capabilities, attract more clients, and increase your earning potential in this evolving field.

CREATIVE WRITING

Making money from creative writing using AI involves leveraging the capabilities of artificial intelligence to enhance your writing process, generate content, or monetize your writing skills. Here's a detailed explanation of how you can achieve this:

1. Writing Assistance: AI can serve as a helpful tool for writers by providing real-time suggestions, grammar and style corrections, and content improvements. Platforms like Grammarly and ProWritingAid use AI algorithms to assist writers in improving their work. While these tools are not specifically designed for creative writing, they can still be useful for enhancing grammar, punctuation, and overall clarity in your creative pieces.

2. Content Generation: AI-powered tools can assist in generating content, such as story ideas, character names, plot structures, and even complete paragraphs or articles. These tools analyze large datasets to identify patterns and generate coherent and original content. GPT-3, the language model underlying ChatGPT, is an example of such a tool. By using AI, you can quickly generate content prompts or storylines to jumpstart your creative writing process.

3. AI-Generated Art: Combining creative writing with AI-generated art can lead to unique opportunities. You can collaborate with AI artists or use generative art algorithms to create visuals that complement your written work. These collaborations can result in unique books, digital art projects, or multimedia experiences that appeal to a wider audience and potentially attract buyers or sponsors.

4. Self-Publishing: With the rise of self-publishing platforms like Amazon Kindle Direct Publishing (KDP), you can publish your creative writing works as e-books or print-on-demand books. Self-publishing provides greater control over your work, higher royalty rates, and access to

a global market. AI tools can help you with editing, formatting, and cover design to enhance the overall presentation of your book.

5. Freelance Writing: AI-generated content has limitations when it comes to creativity and originality, as it often lacks the depth of human imagination and emotion. As a creative writer, you can offer your services as a freelance writer to individuals, businesses, or media organizations. You can write articles, blog posts, copywriting content, or even collaborate with AI-generated content to deliver more comprehensive and engaging pieces.

6. Writing Contests and Grants: Numerous writing contests and grants are available specifically for writers, including those focused on AI and technology. By participating in these contests, you can showcase your creativity, gain recognition, and potentially win cash prizes or publishing opportunities. Some organizations offer grants to writers exploring the intersection of AI and creativity, allowing you to delve deeper into AI-driven writing projects.

7. Writing Courses and Workshops: If you possess expertise in creative writing or have experience working with AI tools, you can create and offer online courses or workshops. These educational resources can teach aspiring writers how to utilize AI for enhancing their creativity, improving their writing process, or exploring new narrative possibilities. Online learning platforms like Udemy or Coursera can help you monetize your knowledge and skills.

8. Sponsored Content and Brand Collaborations: As your creative writing gains recognition and a dedicated audience, you may attract the attention of brands, publishers, or marketers interested in partnering with you. Sponsored content or brand collaborations can include writing stories featuring their products, creating engaging content for their platforms, or producing branded e-books or podcasts. These collaborations can provide financial support and exposure to a wider audience.

Remember, while AI can assist you in various ways, it's important to maintain the unique human touch and creativity in your writing. Embrace AI as a helpful tool, but always strive to bring your own imaginative ideas and emotions into your work.

GHOST WRITING

Ghostwriting involves writing content on behalf of someone else who is typically credited as the author. It is a valuable service for individuals or businesses that lack the time, writing skills, or expertise to create content themselves. AI can be utilized in the ghostwriting process to streamline and enhance the efficiency of creating high-quality content. Here's a detailed guide on how you can make money from ghostwriting using AI:

1. Understanding the Market and Target Audience:
   Conduct market research to identify potential clients and their needs. Determine the industries or niches where you can provide the most value. Some potential clients could be bloggers, authors, website owners, businesses, and professionals seeking content for their websites, books, articles, or marketing materials.

2. Developing AI-Based Writing Skills:

Familiarize yourself with AI-powered writing tools that can assist in generating content. GPT-3.5, the technology behind this AI model, is one such powerful tool. Learn how to effectively use these tools to augment your writing process and improve efficiency.

3. Building a Strong Portfolio:
Create a portfolio that showcases your ghostwriting skills and the content you've created using AI. This portfolio will be crucial in attracting potential clients and demonstrating the quality of your work.

4. Setting Pricing and Service Packages:
Decide on your pricing structure and the types of services you will offer. You may charge per word, per article, or per project. Consider offering different service packages based on the length, complexity, and research required for each project.

5. Marketing and Networking:
Utilize online platforms such as freelance marketplaces, social media, and professional networks to promote your ghostwriting services. Join relevant writing and AI communities to establish yourself as an expert in the field.

6. Client Communication and Collaboration:
   When working with clients, effectively communicate your AI-assisted writing process and set clear expectations regarding the final output. Some clients might be skeptical about AI-generated content, so it's essential to be transparent about the tools you use.

7. Ensuring Quality Control:
   While AI can assist in generating content quickly, it's crucial to maintain a high standard of quality. Review and edit the AI-generated drafts to ensure coherence, accuracy, and alignment with the client's requirements.

8. Offering Specialized Services:
   Consider offering specialized ghostwriting services that cater to specific industries or content types. For example, you could focus on writing technical articles, blog posts for a particular niche, or ghostwriting entire books for aspiring authors.

9. Long-Term Client Relationships:
   Aim to build long-term relationships with your clients by delivering exceptional work consistently. Satisfied

clients are more likely to return for future projects and may refer your services to others.

10. Upselling and Cross-Selling:

Once you have established a relationship with a client, consider upselling additional services such as editing, proofreading, or content strategy consulting. Expanding your service offerings can lead to higher revenue from each client.

11. Staying Updated with AI Advancements:

Keep abreast of the latest advancements in AI and natural language generation. As AI technology improves, new tools and platforms may become available, enhancing the value and capabilities of your ghostwriting services.

Remember that while AI can assist in various aspects of the ghostwriting process, your expertise as a writer and content creator remains invaluable. Balancing the use of AI with your own creative input and editing skills is key to providing high-quality ghostwriting services and building a successful career in this field.

ACADEMIC WRITING

Academic writing using AI can be a lucrative way to make money, as it combines the power of artificial intelligence with the demand for high-quality academic content. Here's a detailed overview of how you can monetize academic writing using AI:

1. Automated Content Generation: AI can be used to generate academic content automatically. You can develop or use existing AI models trained on large datasets to produce essays, research papers, summaries, or other types of academic writing. These AI-generated articles can then be sold or licensed to individuals, educational institutions, or online platforms.

2. Writing Assistance Tools: AI-powered writing tools can assist human writers in producing high-quality academic content. These tools can provide suggestions for sentence structures, grammar corrections, vocabulary enhancements, and even content organization. You can develop or offer these AI writing assistance tools to

students, researchers, or professional writers as paid services or subscription-based platforms.

3. Plagiarism Detection: Plagiarism is a significant concern in academic writing. AI-powered plagiarism detection software can scan academic papers and compare them with a vast database of existing content to identify any instances of plagiarism. You can develop or offer such tools as a service to academic institutions, researchers, or individuals who want to ensure the originality and integrity of their work.

4. Proofreading and Editing: AI algorithms can assist in proofreading and editing academic papers. They can identify grammatical errors, spelling mistakes, and punctuation issues, ensuring that the final document adheres to the required writing standards. You can offer AI-driven proofreading and editing services to students, researchers, or writers looking for professional assistance in polishing their academic work.

5. Language Translation and Localization: AI can also be used for language translation and localization of academic content. You can develop or use existing AI models to

translate academic documents from one language to another, helping researchers and students access information in different languages. This service can be offered to individuals, educational institutions, or publishers working on international academic collaborations or publishing initiatives.

6. Research and Data Analysis: AI algorithms can aid in data analysis and research processes. They can quickly sift through large volumes of data, extract relevant information, and provide insights or summaries. By offering AI-powered research and data analysis services, you can assist researchers, students, or organizations in processing and understanding complex data sets more efficiently.

7. Custom Writing Services: AI can be used to offer personalized academic writing services tailored to specific requirements. By developing AI models that understand user inputs and generate custom content accordingly, you can provide unique and high-quality academic papers to individuals or organizations on demand. These services can cater to various educational levels, from high school to postgraduate studies.

8. Tutoring and Virtual Teaching: AI can facilitate online tutoring and virtual teaching experiences. You can develop AI-powered virtual tutors or teaching assistants that provide personalized guidance and feedback to students. These virtual teaching tools can help students with academic writing, essay structuring, research methodologies, and more. You can offer tutoring services or license the AI tutoring software to educational institutions or online learning platforms.

Remember that while AI can significantly assist in academic writing, it is important to uphold ethical practices. Transparency about the use of AI, ensuring originality, and providing quality content should be prioritized to maintain integrity within the academic community.

RESUME WRITING

Using AI technology, you can create a platform or service that offers automated resume writing assistance to individuals. Here's a detailed breakdown of how you can make money from resume writing using AI:

1. Develop an AI-powered Resume Builder: Build an advanced AI system that can analyze and generate professional resumes. This system should be capable of understanding industry-specific keywords, formatting standards, and best practices for resume writing.

2. Design a User-Friendly Interface: Develop a user-friendly web or mobile application that allows users to input their information, such as work experience, skills, education, and personal details. The interface should be intuitive and guide users through the resume creation process.

3. Implement Resume Templates: Offer a variety of pre-designed resume templates that users can choose from. These templates should cater to different industries, job levels, and preferences. Consider incorporating modern and visually appealing designs to make the resumes stand out.

4. AI-Driven Content Generation: Utilize Natural Language Processing (NLP) algorithms to extract and analyze the user's input data. The AI system can then generate relevant and compelling content based on the provided information, including professional summaries, work experience bullet points, and skill descriptions.

5. Customize and Personalize Resumes: Allow users to customize their resumes by modifying the generated content, rearranging sections, or adding additional details. This feature ensures that each resume reflects the individual's unique qualifications and experiences.

6. Provide Grammar and Spell-checking: Incorporate AI-powered grammar and spell-checking capabilities to ensure that the generated content is error-free and maintains a high level of professionalism.

7. Offer Additional Tools and Features: Enhance the resume writing experience by providing additional tools such as keyword optimization, targeted industry tips, and suggestions for improving the overall effectiveness of the resume.

8. Create Free and Paid Subscription Plans: Offer a free basic plan with limited features to attract users and allow them to experience the service. Additionally, provide premium subscription plans with access to advanced features, exclusive templates, unlimited resume generation, and faster support.

9. Integrate E-commerce Functionality: Implement a secure payment gateway to enable users to subscribe to premium plans or purchase add-on services like cover letter writing, LinkedIn profile optimization, or interview preparation. Offer flexible pricing options, such as monthly, yearly, or one-time payments.

10. Marketing and Monetization: Implement various marketing strategies to promote your AI-powered resume writing service. Utilize digital marketing channels, social media advertising, content marketing, and partnerships with career websites, educational institutions, and job boards. Explore affiliate marketing opportunities with recruitment agencies or other career-focused businesses.

11. Continuous Improvement: Regularly update and refine your AI algorithms based on user feedback,

industry trends, and emerging resume writing best practices. Implement machine learning techniques to improve the accuracy, quality, and relevance of the generated resumes over time.

Remember to consider privacy and security measures to protect user data. Compliance with applicable laws and regulations, such as data protection regulations like GDPR, is crucial.

By combining the power of AI technology with a user-friendly interface and premium features, you can create a profitable business model in the resume writing industry

EDITING AND PROOFREADING

Making money from editing and proofreading using AI involves leveraging the capabilities of artificial intelligence to provide efficient and accurate editing and proofreading services. Here's a detailed explanation of how this can be done:

1. Developing an AI-powered Editing and Proofreading Tool: The first step is to build or utilize an existing AI-powered editing and proofreading tool. This tool should be designed to automatically detect and correct errors in grammar, punctuation, spelling, style, and clarity. It should also provide suggestions for improving sentence structure, vocabulary, and overall readability.

2. Training the AI Model: The AI model needs to be trained using a large dataset of edited and proofread texts. This training data should include both correct and incorrect examples, allowing the AI to learn patterns and develop the ability to accurately identify errors and suggest improvements.

3. Integration into a User-Friendly Interface: Once the AI model is trained, it needs to be integrated into a user-friendly interface. This interface can be a web application, a software tool, or a plugin for popular writing software such as Microsoft Word or Google Docs. The interface should allow users to upload their documents and receive instant editing and proofreading suggestions.

4. Providing Editing and Proofreading Services: With the AI-powered tool and user-friendly interface in place, you can start offering editing and proofreading services. Users can submit their documents through the interface, and the AI will automatically analyze the text, identify errors, and provide suggestions for improvement. Users can review the suggestions and make necessary changes to their documents.

5. Pricing and Monetization: There are several ways to monetize the editing and proofreading services:

   a. Subscription Model: Offer different subscription plans based on usage frequency or the number of words processed. Users can pay a monthly or annual fee to access the AI-powered editing and proofreading tool.

   b. Pay-Per-Use Model: Charge users based on the number of words processed. This model allows users to pay only for the specific documents they want to edit or proofread.

   c. Premium Services: Offer additional premium services such as human editing and proofreading by professional editors. Users who require more in-depth editing or have specialized documents can opt for these services at an additional cost.

d. Enterprise Solutions: Tailor the AI-powered editing and proofreading tool for businesses and organizations that require bulk editing and proofreading services. Offer custom pricing plans and additional features to cater to their specific needs.

6. Marketing and Promotion: To attract customers, implement marketing strategies such as online advertising, content marketing, social media promotion, and partnerships with relevant platforms. Highlight the benefits of AI-powered editing and proofreading, such as faster turnaround times, improved accuracy, and cost-effectiveness.

7. Continuous Improvement: Regularly update and improve the AI model to enhance its editing and proofreading capabilities. Collect user feedback, analyze patterns, and incorporate new language rules, stylistic preferences, and industry-specific requirements into the AI model.

It's important to note that while AI can greatly assist in editing and proofreading, it may not replace the need for human editors entirely. Some complex or nuanced writing may still require human expertise to ensure the highest quality.

TRANSLATION

Making money from translation using AI involves leveraging the capabilities of artificial intelligence technologies to automate and enhance the translation process. Here's a detailed breakdown of how you can monetize translation with AI:

1. Machine Translation Services: AI-powered machine translation (MT) engines can provide quick and automated translations of text, helping individuals and businesses to bridge language barriers. You can build or utilize existing MT models to offer translation services to clients. Monetization can be based on a per-word or per-page pricing model.

2. Post-Editing Machine Translation: While AI can generate translations, they often require human post-

editing to ensure accuracy and quality. You can offer post-editing services, where you review and correct the output generated by machine translation systems. Charging clients for post-editing work can be based on an hourly rate or per-word basis.

3. Custom Translation Models: AI allows you to train custom translation models tailored to specific domains or industries. By building and training such models, you can provide specialized translation services, targeting sectors like legal, medical, technical, or marketing. Charging clients for custom translation models can be a one-time fee or a recurring subscription-based service.

4. Translation API Services: If you have developed or trained translation models, you can expose them as APIs (Application Programming Interfaces). By providing translation API services, you enable developers and businesses to integrate translation capabilities into their own applications or services. Monetization can be based on API usage, with pricing tiers depending on the volume of translations or specific features offered.

5. Localization Services: Localization involves adapting content to a specific language, culture, and locale. AI can assist in automating certain aspects of the localization process. By offering AI-powered localization services, you can help businesses expand their reach to international markets. Monetization can be based on a combination of translation, cultural adaptation, and quality assurance services.

6. Transcription and Subtitling: AI technologies can also be utilized for speech recognition and transcription tasks. By providing transcription and subtitling services, you can convert audio or video content into written text and captions. Charging clients can be based on the length of the audio/video or per-minute pricing for transcription and subtitling work.

7. Language Quality Assessment: AI can be utilized to evaluate the quality of translations by comparing them to human-translated references. You can offer language quality assessment services to clients who require objective evaluations of their translated content. Monetization can be based on the number of translated segments or a project-based pricing model.

8. Language Data Collection and Annotation: AI models require large amounts of high-quality training data. You can monetize the translation process by collecting, curating, and annotating language data for training and improving translation models. Clients who develop AI translation systems may pay for access to such datasets.

9. Consulting and Training: As an expert in AI translation, you can provide consulting services to individuals or businesses interested in implementing AI translation technologies. This can include advising on AI strategy, selecting appropriate tools and models, and offering training sessions on AI translation techniques. Monetization can be based on an hourly rate or a fixed fee for consulting and training services.

10. Content Creation and Localization Platforms: Consider developing a content creation or localization platform that combines AI translation capabilities with user-friendly interfaces. Such platforms can enable clients to create, translate, and manage content efficiently, providing a subscription-based monetization model.

Remember to consider the legal and ethical aspects of translation, respect privacy and confidentiality, and comply with any regulations in your target markets.

FREELANCE BLOGGING

Freelance blogging using AI can be a lucrative way to make money. By leveraging AI tools and techniques, you can enhance your blogging process, improve efficiency, and offer valuable content to your clients. Here's a detailed breakdown of how you can make money from freelance blogging using AI:

1. Identify a Niche: Select a niche that aligns with your interests, knowledge, and market demand. This will help you target specific clients and stand out in the competitive freelance market.

2. Develop Writing Skills: Enhance your writing skills by practicing regularly. Although AI can assist in various aspects, including grammar and spelling, having a strong foundation in writing is crucial to deliver engaging and high-quality content.

3. AI-Based Research: Use AI-powered research tools to gather data and insights. These tools can help you find trending topics, relevant keywords, and statistics to enhance the credibility of your blog posts.

4. Content Creation: AI can be employed to generate content outlines, structure blog posts, and suggest topic ideas. Platforms like Copy.ai and Conversion.ai provide AI-powered writing assistance to speed up the content creation process.

5. Grammar and Proofreading: Utilize AI-based grammar and proofreading tools to ensure your content is error-free. Grammarly and ProWritingAid are popular tools that can help you identify and correct grammar, spelling, and punctuation mistakes.

6. SEO Optimization: Implement AI-based SEO tools like SEMrush or Moz to optimize your blog posts for search engines. These tools can assist you in keyword research, on-page optimization, and tracking the performance of your content.

7. Content Promotion: Use AI-driven social media management tools like Hootsuite or Buffer to automate and schedule your content promotion across various social media platforms. These tools can help you reach a wider audience and increase traffic to your blog.

8. Monetization Strategies: There are several ways to monetize your freelance blogging using AI:

a. Sponsored Posts: Collaborate with brands and businesses to create sponsored content. You can negotiate payment for featuring their products or services in your blog posts.

b. Affiliate Marketing: Join affiliate programs and promote products or services through your blog. When readers make purchases using your affiliate links, you earn a commission.

c. Advertisements: Place advertisements on your blog using platforms like Google AdSense. You earn money when visitors click on the ads displayed on your website.

d. Content Writing Services: Offer your freelance blogging services to clients who require AI-enhanced content. Market yourself as an expert in AI-powered writing techniques to attract clients who value such services.

e. Online Courses or eBooks: Share your knowledge and expertise by creating online courses or eBooks related to your niche. Platforms like Udemy or Amazon Kindle Direct Publishing can help you sell your educational resources.

9. Build a Strong Portfolio: As you complete freelance blogging projects, compile a portfolio showcasing your best work. A well-curated portfolio will demonstrate your expertise to potential clients and increase your chances of securing higher-paying projects.

10. Networking and Branding: Engage in networking activities by attending conferences, joining online communities, and participating in relevant industry events. Build your personal brand by showcasing your expertise, sharing valuable insights, and establishing yourself as a reputable freelance blogger.

Remember, while AI can streamline your blogging process, it's essential to maintain a human touch in your writing to connect with your audience. Balance the use of AI tools with your creativity and expertise to deliver compelling and engaging content.